שִׁשָּׁה

shisha

שֵׁשׁ

six 6 shesh

חֲמִישָׁה יְלָדִים
chamisha yeladim

five children (m)

חָמֵשׁ יְלָדוֹת
chamesh yeladot

five children (f)

חֲמִישָׁה

chamisha

חָמֵשׁ

five 5 chamesh

אַרְבָּעָה נְכָדִים

arba'ah nechadim

four grandkids (m)

אַרְבַּע נְכָדוֹת

arba nechadot

four grandkids (f)

אַרְבָּעָה

arba'ah

אַרְבַּע

arba

four 4

שְׁלוֹשָׁה בָּנִים

shlosha banim

three sons

שָׁלוֹשׁ בָּנוֹת

shalosh banot

three daughters

שְׁלוֹשָׁה

shlosha

שָׁלוֹשׁ

three 3 shalosh

שְׁנֵי סָבִים
shnei savim
two grandfathers

שְׁתֵּי סַבְתוֹת
shtei savtot
two grandmothers

שְׁנַיִם

shnayim

שְׁתַּיִם

two 2 shtayim

אַבָּא אֶחָד

abba echad

one father

אִמָּא אַחַת

imma achat

one mother

אֶחָד

echad

אַחַת

achat

one 1

achat

Achat, shtayim, shalosh,
That's one, two, and three.
Arba, chamesh, and shesh,
That's four, five, six, you see.

Sheva, shmoneh, tesha,
Are seven, eight, and nine.
And finally, there is eser,
That's ten, so get in line!

To take part in our game,
One and all in turn,
Will count achat through eser,
Before we may adjourn.

1 2 3
4 5
6 7
8 9 10

Guide to Transliteration

a ▪ as in barn

e ▪ as in sled

o ▪ as in go

i ▪ as in me

u ▪ as in glue

ei ▪ as in day

tz ▪ in pretzel

ch ▪ as in Loch Ness

or the sound you make
when clearing your throat

More tips:

- Generally, numbers appear before the object they refer to, same as in English.
Example: Ten sons are *asarah banim* (עֲשָׂרָה בָּנִים).

- The one exception to the above rule is for the number ONE, which appears after the object.
Example: One son is *ben echad* (בֵּן אֶחָד).

- The number TWO changes into a combinational form or conjunctive form when it appears before an object.

Example: two sons are *shnei banim* (שְׁנֵי בָּנִים) rather than *shnayim banim* (שְׁנַיִם בָּנִים).

- Specific ordinal numbers exist in Hebrew only for the numbers one through ten.

-- See the charts at the end of the book --

Counting in Hebrew – Important Tips

Counting in Hebrew, as compared with English, may be a bit confusing. There are several major differences between the two languages.

- Numbers in Hebrew are <u>not</u> gender neutral. This is true both for cardinal numbers (one, two, three, etc.) and for ordinal numbers (first, second, third, etc.).

- Numbers in Hebrew are considered to be nouns and therefore can be either in masculine or feminine form.

- Zero in Hebrew is *efes* (אֶפֶס). Since zero is nothing, it does not have a masculine or feminine form. Nothing is, after all, nothing.

- The default form used for counting numbers in Hebrew is the feminine form.

In This Book

- Counting in Hebrew: Important Tips
- Guide to Transliteration of Hebrew Words
- Hebrew Numbers: A Little Rhyme
- Illustrated Guide to Counting From One to Ten
  in Hebrew in Masculine and Feminine Forms

Extras:

- Hebrew Cardinal Numbers From One to Ten
- Hebrew Ordinal Numbers From One to Ten
- Hebrew Words Used in the Book, in
  Singular/Plural, Masculine/Feminine Forms,
  with Transliterations and Translations

Thank you for purchasing
*Counting in Hebrew for
English Speaking Kids*
I hope you enjoy this book!
Shalom!

Author's Note:

Did you know that bilingual children are better at problem solving? This is one of many reasons for exposing your children to more than one language. Multilingual kids have also been found to be better at learning, planning and self-control.

Counting in Hebrew for English Speaking Kids is the second in the series of 'A Taste of Hebrew for Kids' in our Smart Kids Bright Future Children's Books collection. Look out for additional books in the series

Enjoy!

Sarah Mazor

ISBN-13: 978-1495308260
ISBN-10: 149530826X

-

COUNTING IN HEBREW
For English Speaking Kids

by Sarah Mazor

Cover Illustration by Raiza Pascual

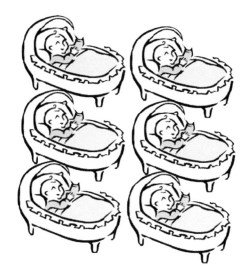

שִׁשָּׁה תִּינוֹקוֹת *

shisha tinokot

six babies (m)

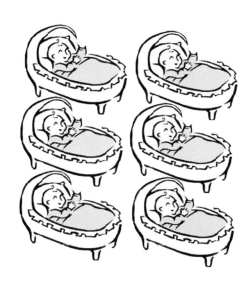

שֵׁשׁ תִּינוֹקוֹת

shesh tinokot

six babies (f)

* Exception to the rule: Both male and female babies are referred to as 'tinokot'.

שִׁבְעָה

shiv'ah

שֶׁבַע

seven 7 sheva

שִׁבְעָה מוֹרִים

shiv'ah morim

seven teachers (m)

שֶׁבַע מוֹרוֹת

sheva morot

seven teachers (f)

שְׁמוֹנָה

shmonah

שְׁמוֹנֶה

eight 8 shmoneh

שְׁמוֹנָה תַּלְמִידִים
shmonah talmidim

eight students (m)

שְׁמוֹנֶה תַּלְמִידוֹת
shmoneh talmidot

eight students (f)

תִּשְׁעָה

tish'ah

תֵּשַׁע

tesha

nine 9

תִּשְׁעָה סוֹפְרִים
tish'ah sofrim

nine authors (m)

תֵּשַׁע סוֹפְרוֹת
tesha sofrot

nine authors (f)

עֲשָׂרָה

asarah

עֶשֶׂר

ten 10 eser

עֲשָׂרָה קוֹרְאִים
asarah kor'im
ten readers (m)

עֶשֶׂר קוֹרְאוֹת
eser kor'ot
ten readers (f)

Hebrew Cardinal Numbers
from One to Ten

English		Hebrew (f)		Hebrew (m)	
one	1	achat	אַחַת	echad	אֶחָד
two	2	shtayim	שְׁתַּיִם	shnayim	שְׁנַיִם
three	3	shalosh	שָׁלוֹשׁ	shlosha	שְׁלוֹשָׁה
four	4	arba	אַרְבַּע	arba'ah	אַרְבָּעָה
five	5	chamesh	חָמֵשׁ	chamisha	חֲמִשָּׁה
six	6	shesh	שֵׁשׁ	shisha	שִׁשָּׁה
seven	7	sheva	שֶׁבַע	shiv'ah	שִׁבְעָה
eight	8	shmoneh	שְׁמוֹנֶה	shmonah	שְׁמוֹנָה
nine	9	tesha	תֵּשַׁע	tish'ah	תִּשְׁעָה
ten	10	eser	עֶשֶׂר	asarah	עֲשָׂרָה

Zero in Hebrew is *efes* אֶפֶס. Since zero is nothing, it does not have a masculine or feminine form.

*See transliteration chart for proper Hebrew pronunciation in the introduction to the book.

Hebrew Ordinal Numbers
from One to Ten

English		Hebrew (f)		Hebrew (m)	
first	1st	rishona	רִאשׁוֹנָה	rishon	רִאשׁוֹן
second	2nd	shniya	שְׁנִיָּה	sheini	שֵׁנִי
third	3rd	shlishit	שְׁלִישִׁית	shlishi	שְׁלִישִׁי
fourth	4th	revi'it	רְבִיעִית	revi'i	רְבִיעִי
fifth	5th	chamishit	חֲמִשִׁית	chamishi	חֲמִשִׁי
sixth	6th	shishit	שִׁשִּׁית	shishi	שִׁשִּׁי
seventh	7th	shvi'it	שְׁבִיעִית	shvi'i	שְׁבִיעִי
eighth	8th	shminit	שְׁמִינִית	shmini	שְׁמִינִי
ninth	9th	tshi'it	תְּשִׁיעִית	tshi'i	תְּשִׁיעִי
tenth	10th	asirit	עֲשִׂירִית	asiri	עֲשִׂירִי

*See transliteration chart for proper Hebrew pronunciation in the introduction to the book.

Hebrew Words in the Book
Singular and Plural

English	Hebrew (Plural)		Hebrew (Singular)	
Father/s	Avot	אָבוֹת	Abba	אַבָּא
Mother/s	Imahot	אִמָהוֹת	Imma	אִמָא
Son/s	Banim	בָּנִים	Ben	בֵּן
Daughter/s	Banot	בָּנוֹת	Bat	בַּת
Grandfather/s	Savim	סָבִים	Saba	סַבָּא
Grandmother/s	Savtot	סַבְתוֹת	Savta	סָבְתָא
Grandchild/ren (m)	Nechadim	נְכָדִים	Neched	נֶכֶד
Grandchild/ren (f)	Nechadot	נְכָדוֹת	Nechdah	נֶכְדָה
Child/ren (m)	Yeladim	יְלָדִים	Yeled	יֶלֶד
Child/ren (f)	Yeladot	יְלָדוֹת	Yaldah	יַלְדָה

Hebrew Words in the Book
Singular and Plural (cont.)

English	Hebrew (Plural)		Hebrew (Singular)	
Baby/ies (m)	Tinokot	תִּינוֹקוֹת	Tinok	תִּינוֹק
Baby/ies (f)	Tinokot	תִּינוֹקוֹת	Tinoket	תִּינוֹקֶת
Teacher/s (m)	Morim	מוֹרִים	Moreh	מוֹרֶה
Teacher/s (f)	Morot	מוֹרוֹת	Morah	מוֹרָה
Student/s (m)	Talmidim	תַּלְמִידִים	Talmid	תַּלְמִיד
Student/s (f)	Talmidot	תַּלְמִידוֹת	Talmidah	תַּלְמִידָה
Author/s (m)	Sofrim	סוֹפְרִים	Sofer	סוֹפֵר
Author/s (f)	Sofrot	סוֹפְרוֹת	Soferet	סוֹפֶרֶת
Reader/s (m)	Kor'im	קוֹרְאִים	Koreh	קוֹרֵא
Reader/s (f)	Kor'ot	קוֹרְאוֹת	Koret	קוֹרֵאת

The End!

Also available

The Hebrew Alphabet for English Speaking Kids

More Hebrew fun books for

English Speaking Kids

Coming Soon!

More Books From the
MazorBooks Library
www.MazorBooks.com
mazorbooks.wordpress.com

Collection of Children's Books with Good Values
- A Bully in Monkeyville. *by Ari Mazor*
- ABC Book of Rhymes *by Mark Eichler*
- Brian Learns to Tell Time *by Mark Eichler*
- Clothes Have Feelings Too! Charlie Learns to Care for His Things. *by Ari Mazor*
- Counting in Hebrew for English Speaking Kids *by Sarah Mazor*
- Go Girl and Little Guy: The Search for Professor Quackers *by Bernardo Juroviesky*
- The Hebrew Alphabet: Book of Rhymes for English Speaking Kids *by Yael Rosenberg and Sarah Mazor*
- I Want to Pet the Ducks: Abey Goes to Washington *by Mark Eichler*
- I Want to Pet the Fish: Abey Visits the Aquarium *by Mark Eichler*
- Little Rose Learns to Count *by Mark Eichler*
- Little Rose's Big Lie *by Shani Eichler*
- Little Shani Learns to Count (Hebrew Edition) *by Mark Eichler*
- Modes of Transportation: ABC Book of Rhymes *by Yael Rosenberg and Sarah Mazor*
- Nurse Olivia "Liv" Welle Presents: Who Knew Vitamins Could Be Fun *by Yael Rosenberg*
- Oh No! There Are Monsters in My Room *by Mark Eichler*
- Positive Affirmations for Little Boys: The ABC Book of Rhymes *by Sarah Mazor*
- Positive Affirmations for Little Girls: The ABC Book of Rhymes *by Sarah Mazor*
- What Will I Be When I Grow Up *by Michali Mazor*

Made in the USA
Lexington, KY
11 August 2014